Brainsluts

Dan Bishop

methuen | drama

LONDON • NEW YORK • OXFORD • NEW DELHI • SYDNEY

METHUEN DRAMA

Bloomsbury Publishing Plc, 50 Bedford Square, London, WC1B 3DP, UK
Bloomsbury Publishing Inc, 1359 Broadway, New York, NY 10018, USA
Bloomsbury Publishing Ireland, 29 Earlsfort Terrace, Dublin 2, D02 AY28, Ireland

BLOOMSBURY, METHUEN DRAMA and the Methuen
Drama logo are trademarks of Bloomsbury Publishing Plc

First published in Great Britain 2026

Cover Design: Em Humble

A catalogue record for this book is available from the British Library.

A catalog record for this book is available from the Library of Congress.

ISBN: PB: 978-1-3506-3924-9
         ePDF: 978-1-3506-3925-6
         eBook: 978-1-3506-3926-3

Series: Modern Plays

Typeset by Westchester Publishing Services

To find out more about our authors and books visit
www.bloomsbury.com and sign up for our newsletters.

Brainsluts

Dan Bishop

SEVEN DIALS
PLAYHOUSE

Brainsluts transferred to Seven Dials Playhouse, London, on 3 February 2026.

From its dynamic, creative hub in the heart of the West End, Seven Dials Playhouse's mission is to nurture theatre-makers and performers at all stages of their careers, and to present innovative live performances enjoyed by diverse audiences.

For Seven Dials Playhouse

Marketing and Communications Manager
Abi Cutler

Technical Manager
Goose Masondo

Duty Managers
Nesmie Constantine
Sas Coumbe
Becca Millar
Grace Wheatley

Front of House Assistants
James Allen
David Anthony
Oscar Chandler
Sas Coumbe
Cranks
Xan Dye
Tobias Engelbrektsson
Eithne Garricks
Zachary Hing
Elihu Ngbodi
Raphael Phillips
Florian Saturley
Luanda Holness

Bios

DAN BISHOP (Writer/Mitch)

Dan Bishop is a writer, comedian and actor from London who studied Writing for Stage and Broadcast Media at Central School of Speech and Drama. His debut comedy play *Brainsluts* sold out its entire run at The Pleasance Theatre at the Edinburgh Fringe 2025, it was short-listed for the Popcorn Writing Award and was a Charlie Hartill Finalist. The play received 4 stars from The Guardian, The Times, The Stage, The List and Broadway Baby.

Dan is also one half of sketch comedy double act Mudfish with Molly Windust. Mudfish were a runner up in the 2024 Sketch Off Final at Leicester Square Theatre and their 2022 Edinburgh Fringe show *Might As Well* received critical acclaim. He can be found online @dansearlystuff.

EMMELINE DOWNIE (Dr Alice Eavis)

Emmeline Downie is a comedian, actor and writer performing across the UK comedy circuit. She co-created and starred in Edinburgh Fringe hits, *Manhunt* and *Manhunt 2: Big Mood*, earning critical acclaim. She's worked on the stand-up shows of comedians such as Ania Magliano, Leo Reich and Bella Hull, and has written for BBC Studios. As well as performing as her alter ego Gail Summerfield, Emmeline plays Louise in Channel 4/A24 sitcom *It Gets Worse* and originated the role of Dr Alice Eavis in *Brainsluts*. She can be found online @actual_emmeline.

KATHY MANIURA (Bathsheba)

Kathy Maniura is an award-winning character comedian, writer and drag performer. Her 2023 Fringe debut *Objectified*, which brought to life a series of surreal objects, earned four award nominations and a successful UK tour. She is about to embark on a UK tour of her latest show *The Cycling Man,* as a middle-aged man in Lycra on the verge of a breakdown, which was named one of the best reviewed shows at the Edinburgh Fringe 2025. A rising star of alternative comedy, Kathy was shortlisted for the BBC New Comedy Awards 2023, is the

Sketch Off Winner 2020 and a So You Think You're Funny? finalist 2021. She is also known for her viral online sketches @kathykathymm.

ROB PRESTON (Duggan)

Rob Preston is a comedian and actor. He has been shortlisted for BBC New Comedian of the Year 2024, Pleasance Reserve 2025 and was a semi-finalist in the Leicester Square Sketch Off 2025. His comedy writing has featured on Radio 4 Extra and he has performed at leading London comedy venues including The Pleasance, Soho Theatre, Up the Creek, Angel Comedy and the Museum of Comedy. He will also appear in Channel 4/A24 sitcom *It Gets Worse* in spring 2026. He can be found online @robpreston_comedy.

BETHAN PUGH (Yaz)

Bethan Pugh is a performer, writer and filmmaker from Leeds. She studied Film Practice at University of the Arts London and her short films have been selected and screened at multiple festivals across the UK. She performs improv comedy at Hoopla and The Free Association, and took part in the Soho Theatre Character Comedy Labs. *Brainsluts* is her first theatre production. She can be found online @bethanpugh_.

NOAH GEELAN (Co-Director)

Noah Geelan is a writer, director, comedian and game designer. As Creative Director at Immersive Gamebox, he has created immersive gaming experiences with Warner Bros, Sony and Netflix. Noah's experiences have been played by over 2 million people worldwide and received a Guardian Culture Pick for theatre in 2023 for 'Squid Game'. Noah has performed around the UK fringe circuit as part of sketch double act Will & Noah, making their Edinburgh Fringe debut at Underbelly in 2025.

SETH JORDAN (Co-Director)

Brainsluts is Seth's first production as director, having worked on a number of productions at the University of Cambridge, including writing the Cambridge Footlights pantomime. Outside of theatre, he works in TV development as a script editor at FIFTH SEASON. He is also currently script editing on the Channel 4 Screenwriting Programme.

ROHAN SHARMA (Associate Director)

Rohan Shamra is a comedian and writer who has been referred to as 'at the very forefront of an exciting new generation of British comedy' by Rolling Stone, and has written for Radio 4 Extra. His debut stand-up hour *Mad Dog* received critical acclaim at the Edinburgh Fringe 2025. *Brainsluts* is his first production as associate director. He can be found online @sharmycomedy.

EDDIE FJ (Sound/Lighting Designer)

For Pleasance Theatre: *Ada and Bron: Origin of Love, Ted Milligan: United.*

Other theatre: *Alex Kitson: This is Water* (Angel Comedy); *Jake Detenber is Gaunty and Flaunty* (Cavendish Theatre); *Matthew Hayhurst: Retirement Show* (Hen & Chickens).

Acknowledgements

The first table read we did of *Brainsluts* was in October 2024. There were many iterations of the cast between then and our opening night in July 2025, and I am incredibly grateful to each actor who gave up their time, energy and thoughts to help me develop the show. So, for those early read throughs and scratch nights, I'd like to thank Ayoade Bamgboye, Marty Gleeson, Bella Hull and Clara Morel.

I am also indebted to the cast and crew who brought *Brainsluts* to life in Edinburgh, those being Emmeline Downie, Kathy Maniura, Bethan Pugh, Rob Preston, Martha West, our director Noah Geelan, producer Gina Donnelly and technician Eddie FJ. The advantage of working with comedians/writers means that, in many cases, they came up with the best lines. I won't say which ones here, in fear it might invalidate my title as writer, but rest assured, the play would have been far weaker without them.

For their notes on the show, their general support and friendship throughout the process I'd like to thank Hannah Afrah, Mojola Akinyemi, Sruti Basak, Amelia Bishop, Carla Borkmann, Paula Borkmann, Esme Bright, Ben Britton, Theo Dick, Jade Franks, Joe Goodman, Agnelle Groombridge, Kate Hiscock, Ollie Lim, Sam McSweeney, Ted Milligan, Eddie Milton-Seall, Clara Morel, Calum O'Toole, Rob Preston, Jaya Rathbone, Leo Reich, Lucy Summerfield and Molly Windust.

Thank you to Sian Carter at Bloomsbury, Em Humble for her amazing poster/cover design, the wonderful team at Chloé Nelkin Consulting, and all the staff at Riverside Studios, The Pleasance (Islington and Edinburgh) and Seven Dials Playhouse (especially Creative Director Katie Pesskin).

And finally, a special thanks must go to two fantastic thinkers/ flatmates, Rohan Sharma and Seth Jordan. Rohan was one of the very first readers of the play, and has helped out until the very end. And, without Seth's patience and encouragement, there would be no *Brainsluts*. He is so clever and cares so much. If you ever get the chance to work with him, you must grab the opportunity with both hands and not let go.

Author's Note

Brainsluts is a slang term used for participants of clinical drug trials. Or so I keep telling people. The truth is, I remember seeing the term and its definition posted on a Reddit thread in 2019, but I've long since lost that Reddit thread and I now can't remember if it even existed.

I wrote the first draft of the play over a one-month period during the summer of 2020. I was a student, it was lockdown, and I remember feeling weirdly hopeful. There was a shifting understanding of which jobs were vital, and which jobs weren't; furlough schemes meant fewer people were working, but they were still getting paid, clearing space for other possibilities of how we might structure our economies; the noise of pollutants was replaced by the sound of birds. Despite the general bleakness of the times, it felt as if what mattered was being reimagined. It was only at the end of the writing process, when I learnt about *The Effect* by Lucy Prebble, that I realised my huge mistake in choosing to set a play in a clinical drug trial, and I decided to put it in a drawer forever.

However, over the next few years, whilst juggling multiple jobs, navigating unpredictable bosses and working unsociable hours, I would catch myself thinking back to *Brainsluts*. Although the play was set in a clinical drug trial, I remembered it being about the gig economy, loneliness and the relationship between the two; something I had a better understanding of now more than ever. Lockdown had become a distant memory, and the sense of potential for something different, engendered by the pause imposed on all our lives, had long been forgotten; it felt like everything had largely stayed the same. I eventually took *Brainsluts* out of its drawer and started redrafting, deciding that more than one play can be set in a clinical drug trial. Please read on to see if you agree.

If you choose to stage a production of *Brainsluts*, update/adapt any cultural references as you see fit, and feel free to swap out funny words for funnier ones.

★★★★

'Audiences may experience considerable changes in brain activity and severe laughter', *The Guardian*

★★★★

'Dan Bishop's witty play could easily be the pilot for a sitcom', *The Times*

★★★★

'Laughs come fast and furious', Lyn Gardner, *The Stage*

★★★★

'A brilliantly funny script and some moments of connection offer a glimmer of hope', *The List*

★★★★

'Brainsluts is comedy with both brains and bite', *Broadway Baby*

Brainsluts

For Mum, Dad and Amelia

Characters

Duggan, *25; easily excitable, there to make friends – optimist.*
Mitch, *26; thinks he's the voice of reason, he's not – noble loser.*
Yaz, *24; anxious to be liked, faultlessly polite – unambitious pragmatist.*
Bathsheba, *30; from a completely different world – believes there's wisdom in the trees.*
Dr Alice Eavis, *28; determined to be positive, easily distracted.*

Note on text: a forward slash (/) indicates interrupted speech; an ellipsis (. . .) indicates a trailing off or a character trying to find the right word.

One

Big white room. The room looks like it belongs to a government-funded institution. There are four chairs and a table. On the table are various magazines (New Statesman, Vogue *etc.*), *a* Good Pub Guide *from 2009, a water jug and some paper cups. Above hangs harsh, white, strip lighting.*

A large, grey noticeboard displaying various NHS posters is fixed to the wall and a red emergency cord hangs from the ceiling. Maybe there's a plant.

Mitch, **Yaz** *and* **Bathsheba** *sit, looking up expectantly at* **Dr Eavis**.

Lights up. Then, immediately:

Dr Eavis (*slightly louder than natural*) Do you all speak English?

Pause. They nod.

That's good! Well not *good* but . . . As in *easier*. And sometimes *easier* is . . . *good*. (*Beat.*) We get all sorts here. (*Beat.*) In a lovely way!

Now. (*Counting.*) One, two, three . . . hmm three. So, one more to go and then there'll be four of you. Four participants, five Sundays. You'll all get to know each other very well.

She smiles. She stops smiling.

Just last year actually, two participants in the same study ended up getting married. So. You never know.

The participants look around at each other; awkward eye contact, weak smiles.

Yaz What drugs were *they* trialling?

Dr Eavis It was a drug for worms.

Mitch   Did the participants already have worms? Or did you have to give them worms?

Dr Eavis   Oh no, all the participants had worms already. The two who got together actually both had a long and vicious history of worms. Probably why they bonded.

She looks at her watch.

We'll get started. Now, I won't be in here the whole time /

Duggan *rushes in, he looks like he's just got out of bed.*

Duggan   Fuck. Sorry. Hi, I'm Duggan. Are you. You're the doctor? Doctor Eavis.

Dr Eavis   Duggan! Yes. I was just settling them in. How are you?

Duggan   Yeah, I'm urm, yeah I'm . . .

Dr Eavis   Brilliant. So, urm, you've read over all the literature we sent you?

Duggan   There was . . . *literature?*

Dr Eavis   No. As in, literature meaning pamphlets? About the trial?

Duggan   Oh right, of course, sorry.

Dr Eavis   And you read them?

Duggan   Of course. Yeah. Yeah. Yes. Yeah. (*He clearly hasn't.*)

Dr Eavis   Good. It's very important that you know exactly what's going to happen.

Duggan   Well I do, because I have read the . . . *literature.*

Dr Eavis   OK. Well if you could just read over and sign this informed consent form that would be great.

Duggan   Oh. Right. Yeah. (*Starts to sign.*)

Dr Eavis   And then this is just a general information one (*Gives him another form.*) so if you could sign that as well . . .

Duggan *does so.*

Dr Eavis   Yes. So. There's cameras there (*Points to left front stage corner of the room.*) and there (*Points to right front stage corner of the room.*) so we can observe you at all times. There's also some magazines but most people just go on their phones, sleep.

She smiles. She stops smiling.

God, it is good that you all speak English. *Easier.* I mean. It's just, I've got another lot next door, and I haven't got a clue what's going on. Must be some sort of language barrier. It was all kicking off earlier – they were *very* angry. *Or* they were celebrating – I couldn't really tell.

She smiles.

Oh! And: the medication! Sorry, it's early. I'm . . . OK. It's over there, (*Points to the table.*) there's two pills: the standard treatment and the new treatment, both in a paper cup each with your name on it. Take them together with water.

Pause.

Sorry, now. Please. I have to watch you take them. So . . . if you could all . . .

Participants all mutter 'oh', 'right', 'yeah' and 'sure'. They start to walk over to the table and take the pills.

Sorry. Just one of those . . . rules.

They swallow the pills.

Brilliant. OK. I'll see you later and we can talk side effects. If you need anything, or there's an emergency. Just pull the red cord.

She smiles. She leaves.

They sit.

Bathsheba *places a plastic bag full of wooden beads on her lap. She starts to thread the beads together using a long piece of string.*

Beat.

Duggan   I'm Duggan by the way.

Mitch   Yeah. You said.

Duggan *nods. Looks around.*

Duggan   Do you . . . have names?

Mitch   Do we *have* names?

Duggan   Yeah.

Mitch   Yeah, I think we all *have* names.

Duggan   Great. That's . . . that's great.

Pause.

Mitch   I'm Mitch.

Duggan   Great.

Yaz   Yaz.

Bathsheba   Bathsheba.

Duggan   Fuck off. Really? Pull the other one.

Bathsheba (*deadly serious, confused*)   Pull the other what?

Duggan   Oh, no. Sorry. I just wasn't expecting. I mean. Bathsheba? That's your actual name?

Bathsheba   Yes.

Duggan   Right. Sorry.

Bathsheba   Don't be sorry. I like my name.

Duggan   Yes, sorry that I . . . sorry.

Silence. **Yaz** *and* **Mitch** *look at their phones.* **Bathsheba** *threads her beads.*

Duggan   So, has anyone done one of these trials before then?

They look around, awkwardly. Then, to break the silence,
Mitch *speaks.*

Mitch   Yeah. I've done my fair share. (*Beat.*) Loads,
actually.

Duggan   Huh. (*Beat.*) Can I ask you something?

Mitch   Sure.

Duggan   Do you ever just like, start dancing or something
to fuck up the results?

Mitch   . . . What?

Duggan   I don't know like start dancing so much that all
the results become invalid?

Pause.

Mitch   What are you saying?

Duggan   You know, just so the scientists have to add to the list
of side effects: may cause nausea, slight swelling and in some
very rare cases it may cause you to dance, dance so much that
you start a whole movement, a whole new way of dancing
that nobody had ever thought of before, a new language of
dance, a dance-language that heals our nation's deep-rooted
divisions. (*Beat.*) You ever done something like that?

Mitch   No, I've not done that, no.

Duggan   And is that something you'd be . . . interested
in trying?

Mitch   Look, sorry mate, I'm not really in the mood to
talk. I just wanna fall asleep, do the tests and get paid. OK?

Duggan   Yeah! Yeah. Of course. *Courrrse* mate. (*Beat.*) No
worries, *gurl*!

You do you. We're here for the long haul so you know. Just.
Hit me up whenever. You know where I'll be.

Pause.

So . . . (*Trying to make eye contact with the others*.) what about you two? Have either of you done a clinical drug trial before?

Yaz   No, this is my first time.

Bathsheba (*still threading her beads*)   I have.

Duggan   Oh, *really*?

Bathsheba   Yeah.

Duggan   Pray tell.

Mitch   You just struggling to get a job?

Bathsheba   No, I've got loads of jobs. I've got a portfolio career.

Yaz   Oh. Right . . . so what do you do?

Bathsheba   Well, I sell my beads on Etsy. Then, two days a week I rent my flat out on Airbnb.

Yaz   Is that . . . legal?

Bathsheba   What's that?

Yaz   Legal? Like, is it against the law to do that?

Bathsheba   Oh, I wouldn't know about things like that.

Yaz   So, sorry, when you rent your flat out, where do *you* stay?

Bathsheba   Oh, I just go for a walk.

Mitch   You go for a walk?

Bathsheba   I love to walk.

Mitch   You go for a *two-day* walk?

Bathsheba   Really clears the mind.

Yaz   Where do you walk to?

Bathsheba   I've done Bedford and back, Bury St Edmunds . . . there's a great car park near me . . .

Mitch   Right.

Bathsheba   But mainly I preach.

Mitch   Do you really?

Bathsheba   Really.

Mitch   As in that's your other job?

Bathsheba   Yeah. I really preach.

Duggan *move closer to* **Bathsheba**. *Maybe he gets up, spins his chair around so the backrest is at the front, and sits back down (like he's a cop interrogating a suspect).*

Duggan   That's wicked! How did you get into that?

Bathsheba   Well, I got speaking to one of those Jehovah's Witnesses one day on my high street, and I just thought . . . Yeah, I could do that.

Yaz   Oh, OK. So, are you like super religious or . . . ?

Bathsheba   Not particularly.

Mitch   Is it good money?

Bathsheba   Pardon?

Mitch   As in, does the preaching pay well?

Bathsheba   Oh. No. Not yet. Soon though. At the moment, they're paying me in exposure.

Yaz   Exposure to what?

Bathsheba   The Lord's teachings.

Mitch   God, that is just everything that's wrong with society today.

Duggan (*trying to impress* **Mitch**)   Organised religion? Tell me about it.

Mitch   No . . . as in, the fact that Bathsheba has to work so many different jobs just to live.

Bathsheba   I love my jobs.

Mitch   Right but, I just think that sometimes, we have a . . . moral duty to turn down the jobs that don't actually need doing. You know?

Bathsheba   Well, if *I* don't rent out my flat on Airbnb then who will?

Mitch   Yeah, but what I'm saying is, you shouldn't have to! (*Beat.*) Anyway. Sorry, I didn't mean to get all sincere, just I happen to know a lot about this topic. This is basically what all my activism's about.

Yaz   Your . . . 'activism'?

Mitch   Yeah.

Yaz   Oh, so you're like . . . an 'activist'?

Mitch   Well, that's a flattering label – but no, I would never call myself an 'activist' per se, but I do my bit.

Yaz   . . . And what is your 'bit'?

Mitch   Well, I mean you guys may not have heard of it, but I've recently become very active in my borough's anti-work movement.

Duggan   Do you mean 'anti-woke' movement, because broski I get you brother, but trust me, whether we like it or not the woke are here to stay.

Mitch   No no – anti-*work* movement. We're a radical political group who believe that no one should have to work if they don't want to.

Yaz   So, does . . . (*Points at everything around her.*) *this* count as work?

Mitch   No, this is *anti*-work. That's why I do so many of these. For me, this is an act of resistance – an act of political resistance!

Bathsheba   Well, that's a very nice thing to tell yourself.

Mitch   No, I'm being completely serious. Why do *you* do so many of these?

Bathsheba   Well, in all honestly, it was my calling. My natural path: my *father* took part in clinical drug trials, *his* father took part in clinical drug trials, his *father's* father . . . That's why the doctors reckon my blood is so thick and creamy.

Yaz   Well . . . (*Making sure she pronounces it right.*) Bathsheba, I'm sorry. That sounds tough.

Bathsheba   Thank you. But . . . it is what it is.

Pause. They all nod in agreement.

Duggan *suddenly feels left out.*

Duggan   Well, all of my doorknobs have fallen off.

They all look at him, alarmed/confused. Long pause.

Mitch   Sorry?

Duggan (*slightly louder*)   All of my doorknobs have fallen 'orf'.

Beat.

Mitch   Oh.

Yaz   OK.

Duggan   They fell off a few months ago now. I can't afford to replace them, so I've just put a sock through the hole where the doorknob is supposed to be and tied a knot at both ends. (*Beat.*) It works alright but it doesn't look great. So, yeah. I need the money too. I need the money to buy some new knobs really. Doorknobs.

Beat.

Yaz   I'm sorry. That must be – you must be in a bad . . . I'm sure things will get better /

Duggan   And an oven. I gotta buy my mum a new oven.

Mitch   Does she not have . . . an oven?

Pause.

I'm sorry, mate.

Yaz   I'm sorry. Things will, things will definitely get better . . .

Beat.

Duggan   Sorry. I don't know why I said all that.

Pause.

Yaz and **Mitch** *get out their phones.* **Bathsheba** *threads her beads.*

Some time.

Duggan (*slightly louder than natural*)   What's the drug we're trialling again?

Mitch   Did you not read the pamphlets?

Duggan   Don't you mean *the literature*?

Mitch   Yes. The literature.

Duggan   No, no. Not me. I like to go into these sorts of things blind.

Yaz   Yeah, but you could be coming out of this sort of thing *blind*.

Duggan *laughs this off.*

Duggan   Not really though.

Yaz   Well, it's a clinical drug trial. There are real risks you should probably know about.

Duggan (*suddenly scared*)   Well, they should have made that A LOT clearer.

Mitch   It'll be fine. I read recently that 'it's more likely you'll get hurt on the way to the trial than as a participant'.

They're just gonna observe us to see if we experience any side effects, that's all.

Duggan   Right. OK. So. I'm not going to go blind?

Mitch   No.

Duggan   Fine. Good. That's fine.

Yaz   Water?

Duggan   Yeah.

Yaz *brings him over a large glass of water.*

Duggan   Thanks.

He downs it. Tosses the empty cup behind him.

Pause. **Yaz** *and* **Mitch** *go on their phones.* **Bathsheba** *threads her beads.*

Duggan   So, we're all just gonna sit on our phones and beads all day then, are we? There was I thinking this would be a great opportunity to unplug, meet new people! You know, like the doctor said, we could meet the loves of our lives here!

Mitch   Yeah, sorry mate, look, I just want to go on my phone . . .

Yaz   I also . . . wouldn't say no to going on my phone . . .

Duggan   Yeah, alright, fine. Fine! Let's not talk. Let's not connect. No need to 'commune'. Let's all just go on our phones and beads all day.

Duggan *slumps.* **Yaz** *and* **Mitch** *go on their phones.* **Bathsheba** *threads her beads.*

Some time. **Duggan** *exhales loudly. Some time.* **Duggan** *starts tapping his foot. Stops. Starts. Stops.*

Yaz   Oh crap.

Mitch   What's up?

Duggan   Trouble in paradise?

Yaz   My 5G's not working.

Mitch   Ah shit, mine's gone too.

Yaz   Bathsheba, is your 5G working?

Bathsheba   Oh, I don't have that. 5G made my nephew infertile.

Mitch   I highly doubt that . . .

Yaz   How old's your nephew?

Batheba (*brightly*)   He's seven.

Duggan (*delighted by the turn of events*)   Well, if all our phones aren't working, I guess we'll all have to spend a little more time with our new pal Duggan then . . .

Yaz *and* **Mitch** *look at each other, slightly horrified.* **Dr Eavis** *bursts in.*

Dr Eavis   I come bearing forms! So, if you could all fill these in and list any side effects you may be experiencing that would be *incroyable*.

Yaz   Excuse me, sorry, but urm do you have the Wi-Fi password?

Dr Eavis   Ooh, yes, I think so . . . yes, what is it again? Uhm, maybe try 'Drugs underscore Trial underscore 123 question mark'?

Mitch   Sorry by 'question mark' do you mean the symbol or you're not sure?

Dr Eavis   Good point, try both!

Yaz *tries.*

Yaz   No . . .

Dr Eavis   OK. Then, uhm, how about 'Drugz' but with a Z at the end?

Mitch *tries.*

Mitch   No, nothing . . .

Dr Eavis   Oh, that's me out I'm afraid – they're my passwords for everything!

She leaves. **Yaz** *and* **Mitch** *look at each other, confused.*

They all gather around the table and take the forms.

Mitch   Seems a bit early in the day to be giving us these forms. We've only just . . . What are you guys – you guys haven't been feeling anything yet, have you?

Duggan   Well, I've got a slight headache.

Mitch   Yeah, but that's probably just in your head though.

Duggan   I'm fairly certain it is in my head, yes.

Yaz   I'm feeling a bit claustrophobic, actually.

Mitch   Hm. Yeah. That might just be the room?

Bathsheba   Well, I definitely think my breasts have gotten bigger.

Mitch   I really don't think they have.

Yaz   Have you been looking?

Mitch   No! I just, I doubt after fifteen minutes Bathsheba's chest has gotten bigger.

Bathsheba   Well, I find with this sort of thing, my breasts tend to be the canary in the coal mine.

Duggan   I'm feeling a bit nervous. I feel like I have an exam in the morning. Do I have an exam in the morning? (*To* **Mitch**.) So you're not feeling anything?

Mitch   Of course not, we literally just got here /

Duggan   No nerves, no stress, no dread?

Mitch   Well, a little bit of dread, yeah. But, if you're not feeling dread, then you're not *really* paying attention . . .

Duggan   I'm gonna write 'dread' down. Does anyone object to me writing 'dread' down?

Mitch   Don't write 'dread' down!

Duggan   All those in favour of me putting 'dread' down say 'aye'.

Yaz/Bathsheba   Aye!

Mitch   No, don't, please! Please don't put anything down. Not yet. These forms are for later in the day, OK? When it kicks in, we'll know about it. (*Beat.*) We're gonna be here for hours.

He looks at them very seriously.

Beat.

Anything could happen.

Lights change.

Dr Eavis *enters and walks downstage. Addresses the audience:*

Dr Eavis   Nothing did happen in the end. No side effects. At one point at 11:16, Duggan thought his hand had gone numb, but then he realised that he had just been sitting on it for over an hour.

At midday they had lunch, it was fine but nothing to write home about. At 2:34 Mitch snuck out for a cigarette, at 4:01 Bathsheba and Yaz yawned at exactly the same time, made eye contact and then quickly looked away. And then, at 5pm, I told them they could all go home.

Duggan asked if anyone wanted to go to the pub.
They didn't.

Week two.

She disappears.

Two

Yaz *is early. She's sat down, staring out, waiting for the others.*

Mitch *comes in, headphones on. He is looking at his reflection in his phone screen and fiddles with his hair. He doesn't see* **Yaz**.

Yaz   Quite uneventful in the end last week . . . !

Mitch *doesn't notice* **Yaz**. *He continues looking at his reflection.* **Yaz** *stands and takes a step closer.*

Yaz   Quite uneventful in the end last week!

Mitch *is startled, jumps back.*

Mitch   Ah! Oh my god!

Yaz   Sorry! Did I make you jump?!

Takes his headphones off.

Mitch   No. I mean, yeah. But it's OK.

Yaz   Sorry!

Mitch   No, it's fine. It's just . . . I'm a jumpy person.

Yaz   Yeah, me too. Oh my god. Yeah. I'm soo jumpy. (*Beat.*) Like one time my ex, he tapped my shoulder on a train, and I jumped up and spilt hot coffee all over a baby.

Beat. **Mitch** *just looks at her. He then starts putting his stuff away in his bag.*

Yaz   Anyway, I was saying – quite uneventful last week really. Like. Not one side effect.

Mitch   Yeah, I felt fine.

Yaz   How was your week?

Mitch   Uhm. Yeah it was good.

Yaz   What did you . . . What do you do when you're not doing this? Apart from the activism.

Mitch   I . . . yeah, I sort of . . .

Yaz   If you don't mind me asking.

Mitch   I'm sort of between things, I don't really /

Yaz   It's OK if you don't wanna say that's /

Mitch   No, no it's cool. (*Beat.*) It's . . . flyering. I'm a flyerer.

Yaz   Oh, cool.

Mitch   Yeah . . .

Beat.

Yaz   What?

Mitch   What?

Yaz   As in, you don't like doing it?

Mitch   Well, I mean it's not what I thought I'd be doing. But yeah, no it's fine.

She looks at him like . . . really?

Mitch   I got that flyering job off Gumtree actually. My job interview was in a containment unit in a Big Yellow Storage. In the unit next door, I heard a man watching *Pointless Celebrities* on full volume. I'm pretty sure he was living there.

Yaz   What do you flyer for?

Mitch   Oh, all sorts. Gyms, restaurants. The company I work for is kind of weird though, like last week they had me flyering for *Little Shop of Horrors* outside a mosque and then yesterday I had to flyer for a halal butcher outside RADA. So . . . (*Moment of realisation.*) Oh wait, actually maybe I did just pick up the wrong box of flyers . . . Yeah, that's on me actually . . .

She laughs. Beat.

Yaz   I haven't had a full-time job for like . . . three years now? The pub near me had two jobs open recently and four-and-half-thousand people applied.

Mitch   Wow. Yeah. I mean I'm not surprised . . .

Yaz   My friend knows the owner and, apparently, he felt so overwhelmed by all the applications that he ended up rejecting everyone and making up the extra shifts himself. He got so exhausted he contracted whooping cough.

Mitch   Whooping cough?

Yaz   Yeah. He had to close down. It's now a Joe & the Juice.

Mitch   Right.

Mitch *nods. Sort of looks in the other direction: he thinks maybe the chat is over.*

Pause.

Yaz   Do you like Joe & The Juice?

He takes a moment to consider the pros and cons of Joe & The Juice.

Mitch   Yeah?

Beat.

Yaz   I applied to loads of studies before I got on this one. FluCamp rejected me because I'm on medication. I thought about going off the medication or lying about being on it but . . .

She trails off. Pause.

Mitch   What about you, how do you . . . 'contribute to society'?

Yaz   What do you mean?

Mitch   As in, what do you do for money?

Yaz   Oh. I'm a structural engineer.

Mitch   Really? Wow.

Yaz   No. (*She laughs to herself, then remains composure.*) I'm a dancer.

Mitch   Oh. That's so cool.

Yaz *smiles to herself. A beat.*

Mitch   Are you actually a dancer?

Yaz   No.

Mitch   Look, you don't have to say if you don't want to.

Yaz   I know.

Mitch   So . . . what do you do?

Yaz   I do nothing.

Mitch   That's OK. Nothing's better than . . . doing something evil.

Yaz   But I'm gonna change that. This is the year that everything changes.

Pause.

Did you get my message by the way?

Mitch   What message?

Yaz   Oh. I uhm. I wanted to ask you something, so I found you online and I . . .

Duggan *and* **Bathsheba** *enter.*

Duggan   Morning all!

Yaz   Morning.

Duggan   Quite uneventful last week in the end, wasn't it?

Yaz   Yeah.

Duggan   Not a single side effect for me.

Bathsheba   Maybe we were the placebo group.

Mitch   Maybe. But sometimes these things just don't . . . kick in.

Dr Eavis *marches in.*

Dr Eavis   Hello! Hello all. Hello Yaz. Are we all . . . ? Yes. We're all here. OK. Brilliant. So. Mamma Mia: Here we go Again! Same as last week, we've got the standard treatment and the new treatment both in a paper cup with your name on it. Any Qs?

Yaz   Oh, actually, yeah did you find out the Wi-Fi password in the end?

Dr Eavis   Ah yes, about that, turns out . . . they're whacking it off for a few weeks. Save a few quid, which is, you know . . . in this economy. Eye roll! Anywhom . . . Take your pills. I'm not gonna watch you this time. Just, I've got to dash next door. Phwwf! Let me tell you! They are. . . . Wow . . . I've never seen anything like it before. It's, it's, it is violent. That's for sure. But it's also . . . beautiful? If you know what I mean. Like, it's *moving* . . . but it's also quite . . . *cruel?* If that makes sense? Anyway, I'll come back at some point later. With something. Probably.

She leaves.

They all go over to the table and take their pills. They disperse. Boredom.

Duggan   Anyone up for a human pyramid?

Mitch   I'm alright.

Duggan   Yaz?

Yaz   Maybe later.

Duggan   Great, I'll check back with you in twenty.

Bathsheba (*to* **Yaz**, *not looking up from her beads*)   So, Yaz. How do you know Dr Eavis?

Yaz   What?

Bathsheba   Dr Eavis said 'Hi' to you specifically. I was just wondering if you had a shared history?

Beat.

Yaz   Oh. Well urm /

Duggan   Did she? That's weird. Why did she do that?

Mitch   Oh yeah, she did say that, didn't she?

Yaz   Oh, it's really nothing, honestly . . .

Mitch   It's not deep, Yaz, but like, yeah . . . do you know her?

Yaz   Well, not really.

Bathsheba   How do you know her?

Yaz   I just know her, you know?

Duggan   Wait, if you know her, isn't that like a 'conflict of interest'?

Yaz   What do you mean?

Duggan (*beat. He's been caught out*)   Oh, I don't know. (*Beat.*) But in my head, it sounded amazing.

Bathsheba   Well, if you know the person running the study that could compromise the results.

Yaz   Well, I mean, 'know' is a strong word. Can you ever *really know*, anyone, *really*?

Bathsheba   What a wonderful question. I think I've only really known one man – a gardener from Czechoslovakia and, truth be told, he came to me in a dream /

Mitch (*to* **Bathsheba**)   OK. OK. (*To* **Yaz**.) But, yeah, go on Yaz, it's fine, just tell us.

Yaz   OK. Fine. But first, um, I just want you to know, I feel really bad about this. Like *really* bad. But urm. My godmother. She's running the study.

Duggan   Doctor Eavis is your godmum?

Yaz   No. My godmother is *running* it, running it. She works for the Contract Research Organisation? It's like the middleman between the drug companies and the pharmacies?

Bathsheba   Oh.

Duggan   OK.

Mitch   What?

Yaz   I know it's stupid but I got this through her.

Mitch   Urm. Yeah. Sorry. I don't think I understand. You got a place on a potentially dangerous, clinical drug trial, through . . . nepotism?

Duggan   You're a nepo baby?

Yaz   Well, sort of, but like I applied just the same way . . .

Duggan (*suddenly chuffed*)   *You're* a nepo baby! I've never met one in the flesh before!

Mitch   And she couldn't have got you a job at reception or something?

Yaz   She didn't want it to come across as completely unfair, and this was the shittiest job they had available.

Duggan   She's risking her goddaughter's health because she doesn't want to seem like a nepotist . . . ? You could go blind!

Yaz   Well, like – it's not *that* dangerous. What did Mitch say? 'It's more likely you'll get hurt on the way to the trial than as a participant.' And the money. The money is good! Two grand for five Sundays? That's *great* money.

This seems to shut them up a bit.

Yaz   So, you don't judge me for getting this through my godmum?

Bathsheba   No.

Mitch   No.

Duggan   It's just . . . weird.

Yaz   Coz I'm as broke as the rest of you. My godmum just pulled some strings coz like . . . she *knew* I was really struggling to get a job. And it was making me like super depressed. Like once I was so depressed that I slept for forty hours straight. Seriously. When I woke up the season was different, the government had changed, my mum had a new haircut. And like even a few weeks ago I was *so* low on money and *so* exhausted that I genuinely even considered signing up for OnlyFans.

Beat.

Bathsheba   What's wrong with OnlyFans?

Yaz   What? Oh, nothing's wrong with OnlyFans . . .

Duggan   Do you think you're better than OnlyFans?

Yaz   No, of course not, I didn't mean it like /

Duggan   Because I've been on OnlyFans, extensively, and trust me, *nothing* is better than OnlyFans!

Bathsheba   Yeah, I love my OnlyFans.

Mitch   Wait . . . *you* have OnlyFans?

Bathsheba   Does that surprise you?

Mitch   Well, no. I mean, yes? What's the right answer?

Bathsheba   It's the easiest money I've ever made. (*To* **Yaz**.) Yaz, you should sell your nudes.

Yaz   Sorry?

Bathsheba   Your nudes. If you're low on money, you should sell them.

Yaz   *My* nudes? (*Trying to play it cool.*) Yeah, I mean, my *nudes* . . . I've been meaning to get round to doing that for uhm . . . yonks.

Bathsheba   Oh . . . do you not . . . have you never sent pictures of yourself?

Yaz (*quickly trying to come up with a lie*)   What? Me? No. I. Big time. I can't stop. I *won't* stop! I . . .

Awkward pause.

Bathsheba   You know there's not even any shame in it anymore.

Yaz   Uh huh . . . !

Bathsheba   I had a job interview last year and they found my account and I thought 'Oh well, there's no way they'll hire me now', but then the interviewer just got out her phone and showed me *her* OnlyFans.

Yaz   Oh my god. That is . . . And sorry, what did they do?

Bathsheba   Mainly nipple play.

Yaz   No, sorry, as in, the company. What did the company that you interviewed for . . . do?

Bathsheba   Oh right. Marketing. I didn't get it.

Yaz   Ah. I'm sorry.

Bathsheba   No, it's OK. Whenever I get rejected from anything, I just take a deep breath in, and remember: I have a body.

Yaz   Oh, right, yeah . . .

Bathsheba   If I'm every strapped for cash, it soothes me to remember that there will always be someone out there who's willing to pay me simply for having . . . a body. I can always life model or do drug trials . . . or join the army! Which suits me just fine. It's just flesh at the end of the day. It has nothing to do with me. Not really.

Yaz   But wouldn't you prefer it if you could make money by like . . . *not* using your body, by like using your mind?

Bathsheba   Why would I want to do that?

Yaz   Because if you just get paid for being a 'body', you're interchangeable, you're sort of nothing. (*Backtracking*.) Or wait, am I being sexist?

Mitch   Bathsheba, it sounds like you should get yourself down to one of our anti-work meetings.

Mitch *reveals some 'ABOLISH WAGE LABOUR' leaflets from his pocket and hands them out to the others*.

Mitch   This week, we're drawing up a definitive list of all the jobs we could just do without.

Bathsheba   Like what?

Mitch   Like consultants, private equity managers, therapy dogs.

Yaz   OK . . . but I'm pretty sure you can't just get rid of whole professions. Like how would anyone make any money if they didn't work?

Mitch   Well, ideally, the government would distribute the wealth evenly and then people could *choose* if they wanted to work or not to like top up their incomes.

Yaz   OK, but like . . . if we all had enough money to live then like . . . *nothing* would ever get done.

Mitch   Exactly! Most things don't need to get done. Our aim is to destigmatise the not doing of things.

Duggan   But I quite like doing things? /

Yaz   OK, but like . . . that would obviously cause economic stagnation.

Mitch   Fine by me – I'm anti-growth.

Yaz   That's not a very smart thing to say. You seriously want us all to get poorer?

Duggan   Yeah, I don't think that's right. You need to grow the economy, if I'm not mistaken. That's just basic . . .

economy. If we grow the pie then everyone gets more pie. Which is great because people love pie!

Mitch   Look, our movement simply believes we need to have a grown-up conversation about the implications of baking such a big pie.

Duggan   Mitch, you're overthinking it. Pie wise, the bigger the better.

Mitch   Well, what if eating such a big pie isn't good for us? What if it's making us all obese and depressed? What if *instead* we bake a slightly smaller pie, that's a little bit healthier, and we make sure that everyone gets a slice?

Yaz   But what about China?!

Mitch   What *about* China?!

Yaz   Well, if we stop growing *our* pie, then how will we ever compete with China? Because, trust me, there's no way the Chinese are giving us a slice of *their* pie!

Mitch   Look, as soon as you bring China into it, you've already /

Duggan (*speaking over them*)   A Chinese pie? I don't think they do pies in China. I think it's more of a wok-based cuisine.

Dr Eavis *enters.*

Dr Eavis   Time for the big weigh-in! And I need a volunteer. 'I volunteer as tribute!' (*She does the three-finger salute from The Hunger Games.*) What's that from? Have I made that up? Yaz, you happy to go first, my love?

Yaz   Uhm, OK. Sure.

Dr Eavis   Lead on, Macduff!

Yaz *leaves the room with* **Dr Eavis** *marching out behind her.*

Beat. **Mitch** *goes to read a magazine.*

Mitch *tries to avoid eye contact.* **Bathsheba** *crosses her legs on a chair, closes her eyes and starts meditating.*

Still thinking about the concept of a Chinese pie.

Duggan (*to himself*)   I guess a bao bun is a sort of . . .

Duggan *looks around the room.*

Duggan (*to* **Mitch**)   Psst.

Mitch   What?

Duggan   Can I tell you a secret?

Mitch   Uhm. OK.

Duggan *beckons* **Mitch** *over.* **Mitch** *acquiesces, tentatively walks over to* **Duggan**.

Duggan (*beat*)   I'm bored.

Mitch *walks away, irritated.* **Duggan** *follows him to sit down.*

Duggan   Bathsheba, what's your favourite /

Mitch   Hey, hey! Shut up. I think she's meditating.

Duggan *peers over.*

Duggan   Woah.

Mitch   How about we just sit here quietly, so we don't disturb her, OK?

Duggan   Well, if she's any good at it, she'll be able to block us out. I've never seen the point in it myself.

Mitch   Well, you could probably do with it, mate.

Duggan   Do you do it?

Mitch   Uhm. A bit. Now and then.

Duggan   Why?

Mitch   It's good, you know . . . it's like good if you have thoughts that you don't like. It's like good at getting rid of some of those bad thoughts. You know?

Duggan   Oh. But I don't have bad thoughts. I have cool thoughts. Like sometimes I think no one is thinking about as cool stuff as I am.

Mitch   OK. Good for you.

Duggan   Like right now I'm thinking of a . . . (*Tries to come up with a 'cool thought'. The actor should improvise a new 'cool thought' each night if they want to.*) a room full of knives (*Happy with his 'cool thought.'*) That's cool.

Mitch   Yeah, but I guess I mean like bad thoughts as in *intrusive* thoughts . . .

Duggan   Or like right now I'm thinking about blind guide dogs playing football, and, credit to them, they're just getting on with it and . . . it's really fucking nice actually.

Mitch   You do know that's not what I mean, right?

Bathsheba (*still with her eyes closed*)   Shhhh.

Mitch   Sorry, Bathsheba. (*Turns to* **Duggan**.) Shh!

Beat.

Duggan   Bathsheba, can we have a go?

Bathsheba   Oh. Urm. Well, it's more of an internal thing. It helps me calm down.

Duggan   But it might be quite nice to do it all together . . . ?

Mitch   Duggan, the woman wants to be left alone.

Duggan   You don't know that. Bathsheba?

Bathsheba (*beat, she thinks about it*)   OK.

Beat.

Duggan   OK! So, how does this work then?

Bathsheba   Well, I want you to put your hands on your knees and to close your eyes.

They do so.

Take a deep breath in.

They do so. **Bathsheba** *pauses for a few seconds.*

And out.

Now I want you to imagine that you're walking along a beach. You can feel the hot sand beneath your feet, the bright sunlight warming your neck and you can hear the waves lapping against the shore.

Now breathe in, and breathe out.

Duggan *starts squirming.*

Bathsheba   Duggan, I can sense there's some tension in your body. Try and relax your whole being.

Duggan   Sorry, it's just. I can't stand the beach. (*He opens his eyes.*)

Bathsheba (*with her eyes still shut*)   Eyes shut, Duggan.

Duggan *shuts his eyes again.*

Duggan   Sorry.

Mitch   What's wrong with the beach?

Duggan   Well, it's just the sand, it gets everywhere. In your hair, in between your toes /

Bathsheba   OK, well, then I want you to imagine that you're walking along a small stone path *away* from the beach, directly into the woods.

Mitch   Wait, sorry, am I still barefoot at this point? Just, I'm imagining stepping on a lot of pine cones and that's sort of taking me out of it.

Bathsheba (*slightly annoyed, but regaining composure*)   OK, well. . . . then, by the side of the path, you find a beautiful pair of . . . (*Trying to think of something.*) Leather clogs.

Duggan   Clogs? I don't want clogs.

Bathsheba (*slightly more annoyed now*)   OK, you find some footwear of your choice then. (*Retaining her Zen.*) And you slip them on.

Duggan   Can I have cowboy boots?

Bathsheba *sighs.*

Bathsheba   Yes, you can have cowboy boots.

Duggan   I know that being a cowboy is so much more than the boot, but I've just always wanted a pair, so thank you.

Bathsheba   You hear the rustling of the leaves. And you can smell the sweet scent of summer flowers on the breeze.

Mitch   Just gonna stop you there Bathsheba, I actually suffer from medical grade hay fever.

Bathsheba (*snapping now*)   OK, well maybe we should just all do our own meditations.

Duggan   *Or*, how about we all do a line each?

Bathsheba (*really trying to retain her Zen now*)   OK. Fine. That's fine.

Duggan   Do you want to start, Bathsheba?

Bathsheba   OK. (*She breathes in.*) I want you to imagine that you're walking through a . . . desert.

Duggan   Sand.

Bathsheba   Sorry. (*Beat.*) A field.

Mitch   Hay fever.

Bathsheba   Sorry. A . . . big . . . Tesco.

Duggan/Mitch   Mmm.

At some point in the next three lines **Dr Eavis** *and* **Yaz** *return and silently watch the meditation unfold.*

Bathsheba   You can feel the cool breeze of the . . . pork fridge on your face. And you can hear the sounds of children laughing . . . in the 'world foods aisle'. You bump into an old friend and hug them tightly. In their warm embrace you feel connected to the universe. (*Beat.*) Mitch, would you like to continue?

Mitch   Uhm. Yeah. OK. (*Trying to imitate* **Bathsheba***'s Zen voice.*) The old friend whispers in your ear. They tell you they love you. They tell you they forgive you. They tell you they're dying. That they've been dying for years and that it's all your fault. They tell you they forgive you again. They then kiss you on the forehead and immediately turn to ash in your hands. (*Beat.*) Duggan?

Duggan (*beat. He's thinking . . .*)   You scoop up the ash. And you put it in your pocket. It's a bit like sand. Yuck. You are completely present. You have no future. You have no past. You don't know where you are. You are possibly suffering from amnesia, and that makes you feel . . . epic.

Dr Eavis   Sorry, but what's going on . . . ?

Duggan, **Mitch** *and* **Bathsheba** *startle – their eyes open and their legs uncross.*

Mitch   Oh, hi. Sorry. You weren't supposed to see that. We were just, we were urm . . . we were . . . /

Bathsheba   It's actually an ancient meditative practice . . . /

Duggan (*louder than natural*)   We were just getting rid of the bad thoughts.

Beat.

Lights change.

Dr Eavis *walks downstage. Addresses the audience.*

Dr Eavis   After lunch, Duggan fell asleep in a corner. That was at 1:32. At 1:37, Yaz and Mitch tore up little squares of paper, wrote letters on them and tried to play a game of Scrabble on the floor. They asked Bathsheba if she wanted to join, but she politely declined. At 5pm, I told them they could all go home. As they were getting their things, I overheard Mitch ask Yaz if maybe she'd want to go for a drink sometime.

Beat.

Week three.

She disappears.

Three

All the participants are sitting on the floor or on chairs, doubled over, in pain. They are all wincing, breathing deliberately, trying to make the pain go away.

Duggan   Jesus-fuck this hurts!

Mitch   I've done loads of these before, and I've never felt pain . . . (*Winces in pain.*) as bad as this.

Yaz *starts squeezing* **Mitch***'s hand very tightly.*

Yaz   Stop squeezing my hand!

Mitch   You're squeezing *my* hand!

Yaz   Only because you're squeezing *my* haaand!

Duggan   Will you two stop being so handsy!

Mitch   We're not being handsy!

Bathsheba   Well, sex is a very effective pain relief. Even hand stuff.

Mitch   Surely not hand stuff?!

Yaz   Has anyone pulled the red cord?!

Duggan   I pulled the red cord ages ago!

Dr Eavis *walks in as if addressing a huge crowd of adoring fans.*

Dr Eavis   Glastonbury! Are we well?!

Yaz   We're in a lot of pain, all of us, in our stomachs.

Mitch   The new drug this week, something's wrong. I've done loads of these before and something's definitely wrong.

Duggan   Give us some painkillers /

Yaz   *Strong* painkillers please!

Dr Eavis   Oh no! I'm sorry but we can't give you any pain relief because it might interfere with the results of the trial. That *was* in the literature.

Duggan (*finally confessing, still writhing on the floor*)   I didn't read the fucking literature!

Dr Eavis   How about I go and get you all a hot water bottle?

Mitch   A hot water bottle?!

Dr Eavis   Or a cold compress?

Mitch   No!

Dr Eavis   Or you might all just be a bit . . . peckish? I'll tell you what, I've got a tangerine in my bag. Why don't you just stay here, and I'll go get that. Don't move a muscle!

Dr Eavis *rushes out.*

Mitch   Where is she going?!

Duggan   Yaz, what's the point in being a neop baby if you can't get us some pain killers!

Yaz   I'm *not* a nepo baby!

Bathsheba   Everyone, please, listen to me! We all just need to put ourselves in the recovery position. Trust me.

Mitch   No, please, I really think we should just wait for Dr Eavis.

Bathsheba   Come on everyone, everyone down!

They all lower themselves to the floor.

Yaz   What is the recovery position again?

Bathsheba   Well firstly, it's your left side.

Yaz *turns over.*

Bathsheba   And then you put your left leg up like you're kneeing something /

Duggan   What am I kneeing?

Bathsheba   Then your right leg goes up in the air, you extend your left hand forward and with your right hand, you firmly clasp your rump.

Everyone does so.

Bathsheba   Has everyone got that?

Mitch, **Yaz** *and* **Duggan** *all groan in pain.* **Bathsheba** *looks over at their various positions.*

Bathsheba   Doesn't look quite right. (*Beat.*) Maybe it is the right side.

Dr Eavis *enters.*

Dr Eavis   Oh my god, you're gonna hate me! I've already eaten my tangerine for lunch! (*Suddenly notices everyone on the floor.*) Oh. Is everything OK?

Bathsheba   Don't worry, Doctor. Everything's under control. I've put everyone in the recovery position.

Mitch   No! We're all still very much in pain!

Dr Eavis   OK. Well. Unfortunately, if it's just a stomach pain, there's not much I can do for you at the moment. How about I get you those forms and you can write down exactly what you're feeling? That might make you feel better.

They groan. She leaves.

Yaz   I'm not sure how much more of this I can take.

Bathsheba   I think we'll all be fine if we just practise some mindful breathing . . .

Yaz   How d'you do that?

Bathsheba   So, if we just start with Downward Dog. So that's feet on the floor, palms on the floor, bum in the air.

They do so.

And breathe . . .

They breathe.

Then into the Foetal position . . .

They do so.

And breathe . . .

They breathe.

Then into Foetal Dog.

Mitch   Which one's that?

Bathsheba   Copy me.

Bathsheba *sits on her knees, places her forehead on the floor, lets her arms rest behind her with her palms faced up. They copy her.*

Bathsheba   And breathe in . . .

They breathe in.

Yaz   Wow, I can't believe that's actually working.

Bathsheba   And breathe in. . . .

They breathe in.

Duggan   I'm breathing in quite a lot of floor!

Bathsheba   And . . . breathe in . . .

Mitch   In again?!

Duggan   I'm full!

Bathsheba   And breathe out . . .

They all exhale violently. After a moment:

Mitch   Oh, yeah that's not bad actually . . .

They start to stand up. **Duggan** *picks up a magazine.*

Yaz   Yeah, I actually feel so much better.

Mitch (*touching her shoulder*)   You OK? I was worried about you for a second there.

Yaz *smiles.*

Yaz   Thanks. I was worried about you too. Water?

He nods, she goes to get water. **Bathsheba** *has adopted a new yogic pose.*

Duggan   Why is this magazine in Korean? I thought I'd read all the magazines but this one, it's in Korean.

Mitch   That's not Korean, Duggan.

Duggan   Oh. Sorry. Is it . . . Kanji? Mandarin?

Mitch   No, Duggan, that's more that . . . well, that's in English.

Duggan   English? I know English. This is not English. Wait, everything's gone . . . Blurry.

Yaz   Have you? Oh my god. You've lost your vision. (*To the others.*) He's lost his vision.

Bathsheba   Oh dear.

Mitch   Oh shit.

Duggan   I've gone blind! Mitch, you promised me I wouldn't go blind!

Mitch   Duggan's lost his vision! OK, everyone, prepare for eyesight shut down. (*Turns to* **Bathsheba**.) Yaz, get him some water.

Bathsheba   I'm not Yaz.

Mitch   That's mine gone.

They start freaking out.

Pull the red cord, we need to pull the red cord!

They scramble around trying to find the red cord.

Yaz *yelps.*

Yaz   That's my hair!

Duggan   Fuck. Sorry!

Bathsheba (*freezes*)   What's that noise?

They all freeze.

Mitch   What noise?

Bathsheba   That sort of . . . continuous yelping crow noise. Is there a crow in here?

Mitch   Who let a bloody crow in here, that's going to muck up the results!

Yaz   Duggan, did you let a crow in here?

Duggan   I'm blind, I can't hear anything!

Bathsheba   It's like a 'graww graww graww graawwww'.

Duggan   Oh! Now I hear something!

Yaz   No, Duggan, she was just making the noise!

Duggan   Oh, well tell her to stop. I can't hear the original crow noise!

Yaz   Bathsheba, stop making that stupid crow noise!

Bathsheba   I have stopped.

Yaz   You literally haven't! (*The penny drops.*) Ah, I think we can all hear the crow now.

They flinch in unison in relation to the crow.

Mitch   OK, well we may not be able to see and we might all be collectively hallucinating a giant crow –

Duggan   I'm actually imagining a number of very small crows –

Mitch   But, at least the pain in our stomachs has gone, right?

Beat. **Mitch** *spoke too soon: the pain is back. They wince and groan in unison and start breathing very deliberately.*

Bathsheba   OK everyone, let's move back into Foetal Dog.

They all try to feel their way down to the floor and get into Foetal Dog, loudly breathing through the pain. **Dr Eavis** *marches in with some forms.*

Dr Eavis   Speeeeding round the corner with some *Form*-ula 1s for you! (*Beat.*) Oh. You're all still here. Right. Well. You do you. I ain't gonna yuck your yum! I'll leave these forms here and you fill your filthy boots.

She turns to leave.

Yaz   We need a doctor!

Dr Eavis *turns back, walks towards* **Yaz**.

Dr Eavis   Well, that's what the lanyard says. How can I help?

Yaz   No, you know, a *proper* doctor! We're all in *serious* pain!

Dr Eavis   What do you mean a 'proper' doctor, I am a *proper*, *qualified*, doctor.

Yaz   You're really not taking this seriously!

Dr Eavis   You know, next door's group don't speak to me like this!

Mitch   Next door's group *can't* speak to you . . . at all!

Yaz   Please, just get someone else /

Dr Eavis   I am not getting paid enough for this /

Mitch   Don't get upset, just go get us a second opinion!

Dr Eavis   I *am* the second opinion! (*Beat.*) Listen, I'm not supposed to know this, OK, but I may have 'accidentally' seen the 'proper' doctor's notes for this week's trial, and guess what, *this* week is the placebo!

Pause.

The pain subsides, the vision returns, the noises stop. They look sheepish.

Lights change.

Dr Eavis *walks downstage. Addresses the audience.*

Dr Eavis   That really fucked me off actually.

After that, they all stayed quiet for a bit. Then at 2:24pm, they made small talk. Mitch said they should all write to their MPs about data mining. Bathsheba denounced God. You get the gist.

At 3pm they all slept. In a little row on the floor. It was quite sweet actually. Well, Bathsheba, Duggan and Mitch slept. Yaz just lay there. At one point Mitch repositioned himself and his foot sort of touched her leg. She thought about kicking it off, but then she decided not to.

Week four.

She disappears.

Four

*Yaz and **Mitch** are sitting next to each other. A moment, then **Duggan** enters.*

Duggan   Morning perverts!

Yaz   . . . morning.

Duggan   Good weekends, I trust?

*Mitch and **Yaz** notice that there's writing all down **Duggan**'s arm.*

Yaz   Duggan, what is that all down your arm?

Duggan   Well, I was wondering when you were gonna ask . . .

Mitch   You literally just got here /

Duggan   Let me explain. (*Beat.*) The meals they give us here, they're dogshit, right?

Yaz   Urm . . . they're not that bad . . .

Mitch   I quite like the food here . . .

Duggan   Trust me – they're dogshit. Anyway, you know the posh pizza place across the road? Today, I thought: instead of eating all that dogshit medical research food, we order in.

*Although **Duggan** is satisfied that that's an adequate explanation, the others aren't . . .*

Mitch   OK . . .

Yaz   But that doesn't explain . . .

Mitch   The writing?

Duggan   The what?

Mitch   The writing down your arm, Duggan /

Duggan   Oh, yeah! So, my thinking there was: as there's still no Wi-Fi, I won't be able to get the menu up on my phone, *so* I decided to go into the restaurant, copy out the menu onto my arm, and now we can all order off here.

Duggan *presents his arm.*

Pause.

Yaz   Why didn't you just take a picture of the menu on your phone?

Mitch   Or just take a menu?

Duggan *realises his mistake.*

Duggan   Look, do you want pizza or not?

They both gather round his arm. They're struggling to read his handwriting.

Mitch   Your handwriting's awful . . .

Duggan   I wrote it with my left hand!

Yaz/Mitch   . . . Why?

Duggan   I don't know!

Yaz   Urm . . . Probably just a margherita for me.

Duggan   A margherita? You can't get that! Look – this place is the real deal – they've got (*Reading off his own arm.*) sausage and pesto, spinach and blue cheese – they're serving artichoke and jam . . . (*Confused, to himself.*) Artichoke and jam? (*He rolls up his sleeve a bit more.*) Artichoke and jamón, for fuck's sake!

Mitch   Margherita for me too, please. Cheers, mate.

Duggan   Jesus Christ. Fine.

He takes out his phone, starts to call the pizza place. It's ringing.

I can't believe this – you two have really brought a knife to a bun fight on this one.

Mitch   . . . What was that you just said?

Yaz   Did he just say, 'a knife to a *bun* fight'?

Duggan (*to* **Yaz**, *annoyed*)   Yeah, it's a phrase. (*On phone, delighted.*) Hello! Is this Emilio's Pizza Emporium?

Mitch   That's not the phrase . . .

Duggan (*to* **Mitch**, *annoyed*)   It *is* the phrase! (*On phone, delighted.*) It is? Fantastic! Come stai oggi?

Mitch   Why would that be the phrase? What could that *possibly* mean?

Duggan (*on phone, delighted*)   Well, felice di sentirlo! (*To* **Mitch**, *annoyed.*) It means, it, it means, y'know, here I am trying to have a nice bun and you've brought a bloody knife . . . like *what?!* What have you done that for, you prick?!

Mitch   Why would there be a phrase for that?!

Yaz   It's not a phrase . . .

Duggan (*to* **Yaz**, *annoyed*)   It *is* a phrase! (*On phone, delighted.*) I would like *uno* artichoke and jamón – yes, I thought it was a good choice too – and *due* margheritas if you please – I know, I know . . . I tried to talk them out of it – with all this choice I know, yeah exactly – it *is* like bringing a knife to a bun fight! (*He laughs down the phone.*) Oh sorry, one second . . . (*To others.*) Bathsheba, what do you want?

They all look around.

Duggan   Where is Bathsheba?

Yaz   Yeah . . . where is Bathsheba?

They can't see her.

Duggan (*on phone*)   Sorry, yeah that's everything. Great. Grazie mille. Cheers, Emilio. (*Beat.*) Oh, there is no Emilio. (*Beat.*) So, to whom do I owe the pleasure? (*Beat.*) Ryan? That's amazing. (*He hangs up. To the others.*) That was Ryan.

They look at each other . . . slightly concerned.

Yaz   So . . . where is Bathsheba?

Mitch   Well, it's only just gone ten. She's probably just running /

Dr Eavis *marches in.*

Dr Eavis   Hello. One, two, three . . . Where's . . . where's Bathsheba?

Yaz   We don't know.

Dr Eavis   Hm. OK. That's. Urm. I'll give her a call.

Turns to leave, then turns back out of politeness.

How was everyone's weeks? OK?

They nod.

Phone consultations . . . happened? (*Beat.*) All fine? Fine.

She leaves. Beat.

Yaz   Do you think something's happened to Bathsheba?

Mitch   As in . . . ?

Yaz   You don't think it was last week's pill, do you?

Mitch   No . . . 'It's more likely you'll get hurt on the way to the trial than as a participant'. She'll be running late.

Yaz   OK. (*Reassuring herself.*) Yeah. And last week was . . . the placebo anyway.

Mitch   Exactly.

Yaz   Hm.

Mitch   What is it?

Yaz   I don't know.

Mitch   What were you gonna say?

Yaz   I mean . . . what if . . . it *wasn't* the placebo?

Mitch   But she told us it was . . .

Yaz   Yeah. She *told* us that. And when she told us that, our pain went away. But maybe *that's* what was in our heads. If we expect to feel pain, we feel pain. But if a doctor tells us we're not in pain, the pain goes away. Maybe?

Mitch   Yaz, this isn't some big conspiracy.

Yaz   And sort of bigger than that is like, you know, she's really not allowed to know, that kind of information won't just be lying around. I talk to my godmum about this stuff and she doesn't even know which one's the placebo until weeks after the trial and she's in charge. (*Beat.*) Or maybe she was just trying to fuck with us.

Mitch   No, it was all in our heads. Being in this room, it's just making us all go a bit . . . loopy.

Yaz   Yeah, you're probably right.

Duggan (*tentatively*)   I mean . . . I wasn't going to mention it, but my pain did come back a few times in the week.

Yaz   Really?

Duggan   Yeah?

Yaz   Same. I had exactly the same pain come back three or four times in the week.

Mitch   Are you guys sure? Like Duggan, you probably just ate something weird, and Yaz, maybe you were like on your period?

Yaz   That's a strange thing to say.

Duggan   Yeah, why would you presume that I ate something weird?

Yaz   I think, if we both felt pain in the week, maybe something was wrong with last week's pill. And maybe, that's why Bathsheba's not here. Maybe something happened to her.

Duggan   What? What happened to her?

Mitch   I felt fine during the week – it's *so* unlikely that something's happened /

Yaz   But it *does* happen. My godmum has told me some stories /

Duggan   Don't say stuff like that!

Mitch   She'll be here!

Beat.

Dr Eavis *marches in.*

Dr Eavis   Hi. Everyone listening? OK. Unfortunately, we're going to have to stop the study for today.

Yaz   Why?

Duggan   Has something happened?

Yaz   Did something happen to Bathsheba?

Dr Eavis (*taken aback by the flood of questions*)   I'm not at liberty to give you that information; it would breach patient/doctor confidentiality.

Yaz   Was it last week's pill?

Dr Eavis   I'm not at liberty to give you that information /

Yaz   But what if the same thing that's happened to her, happens to us?

Dr Eavis   I am not at liberty to tell you whether something has happened or has not happened to her. The same rules apply, if you experience any unusual side effects throughout the week which you believe to be in relation to the study then call the hotline.

Yaz   Why are you speaking like this?

Dr Eavis   Speaking like what?

Yaz   You're speaking in that like medical, passive, tone way. It's not – I don't like it.

Dr Eavis (*rising to the bait*)   I'm very sorry you feel that way.

Yaz   You're not even a proper doctor.

Dr Eavis   I am a proper doctor.

Beat.

We'll be in touch about whether the rest of the trial will go ahead or not. And . . . regarding payment, you'll only be paid for the weeks you've completed.

Mitch   Wait. Sorry, so we're not getting paid for this week?

Dr Eavis   No.

Mitch   Right. Well, um, that's really not . . . /

Dr Eavis   We're sorry for the inconvenience.

Mitch   Yeah, fucking inconvenient actually, yeah!

Yaz   I know last week wasn't the placebo. That was a lie. You lied to us.

Dr Eavis   I'd like to remind you that this conversation is being recorded and could affect the results of the study.

Yaz   I could tell someone. I could tell my godmum you know.

Pause.

Dr Eavis (*to* **Yaz**)   At this facility we do not tolerate any sort of harassment, verbal or physical.

Beat. To everyone.

We'll be in touch. Goodbye.

She leaves.

Pause.

Mitch (*under his breath*)   Fuck's sake.

Yaz   Hey, it's OK. She'll be OK.

Mitch   Who'll be OK?

Yaz   Like you said before, Bathsheba will be fine.

Mitch   Oh, no. I don't care about that. Did you not hear her? We're not getting paid for this week.

Yaz   Oh. OK. But like . . . Bathsheba could be hurt?

Mitch   That's not my priority. My priority is getting paid. I don't want Bathsheba to die or whatever but . . . I don't really know her. I need the money.

Yaz   And so do I.

Mitch   Yeah. OK.

Yaz   What? I do . . .

Mitch *looks at* **Duggan**.

Yaz   What's that look, what does that mean?

Mitch   Nothing. That look means nothing.

Yaz   No, it means something. What do you mean?

Mitch   OK, it's just like . . . How much do you need the money, *really*? Like if your godmum works for a drugs company or whatever, that's pretty lucrative.

Yaz   Just because she's my godmum doesn't mean I have any connection to *her* money.

Mitch   OK, but like, your dad has a nice car.

Yaz   What?

Mitch   Like when you left mine this week, outside my flat, your dad pulled up in a . . . really nice car.

Duggan   Why were you in his flat?

Yaz (*to* **Mitch**)   Why are you saying this?

Duggan   Are you two seeing each other?

Mitch   I'm just saying that you presented yourself as if you're struggling for money as much as the rest of us or whatever and then your dad has, I don't know cars, but it's it's it's it's silver.

Yaz   Well firstly, the colour obviously has no relation to the value of the car . . . and also, sorry, but you live in a flat by yourself. How the fuck do you afford that on a flyerer's salary?

Mitch   Well, if you must know, someone died. So yeah, I really lucked out there.

Yaz   OK. (*They both think the conversation has ended. But* **Yaz** *can't help herself.*) But . . . I mean, what did *they* do for a living?

Mitch   Well, that is none of your business.

Yaz   They must have had a bit of money, were they a banker or something?

Mitch   OK, I'm not gonna answer that. But, you know, Karl Marx's dad was a corporate lawyer so, yeah, some of the most left-wing people *ever* are related to corporate lawyers you know! /

Yaz   I just don't get how you can care more about getting paid than if our friend is hurt? Like, you're a socialist, aren't you? You're all about 'anti-growth' and 'sucking off Trotsky'.

Mitch   I am a socialist, but like, I still need to eat!

Yaz   Then get a proper job instead of spending all your time lecturing people about how unfair everything is!

Mitch   I'm sure you appreciate that I wouldn't be here if I could get a job doing anything else!

Yaz   And neither would I! God, you're so annoying, I can't believe I let you fu /

Mitch   Woah! 'Let you'? Let's not say 'Let you'! And also, I am NOT annoying!

Yaz   Oh, just fuck off!

Mitch   *You* fuck off!

Duggan (*slightly louder than normal*)   My doorknobs haven't fallen off.

Silence.

Mitch   What?

Duggan   My doorknobs. They're still attached. They haven't fallen off. I lied.

Pause.

Yaz   Wait, I'm confused.

Duggan   I work in recruitment. And my doorknobs haven't fallen off. They're still attached.

Pause. **Yaz** *and* **Mitch** *look at each other.*

Duggan   I work in recruitment recruiting recruiters for other recruitment firms. It's fucked.

Beat.

Mitch   Why are you telling us this?

Pause.

Duggan   Because, I don't need the money. Not really. Not like you two. The real reason I signed up for this study is because I . . . was lonely. (*Beat.*) Slash: a little bit bored. That's why I'm here. (*Beat.*) And I was sitting in Starbucks a few weeks ago and I overheard this man telling this woman that all his doorknobs had fallen off and he had used a sock tied at both ends to shut and open his doors and he wanted to buy his mum a new oven and they were on a date I think or they had met on an app where people who have moved to a new place meet up and talk about that place and and and from his coffee cup I could see that his name was Torn.

Beat.

Yaz   Torn?

Duggan   Yeah. T.O.R.N. Torn.

Mitch   Probably Tom.

Beat.

Duggan   And I overheard what Torn was saying and I
thought I could say the doorknob thing to people and they
might like me because I thought I don't know it might be
an interesting thing to . . . say? But now I'm here, I can
see how fucked it all is. That people have to do shit like *this*
and now Bathsheba could be like . . . hurt. But I've been
thinking, if it was like jury duty, if this whole thing was like
that, then everyone would have to do it whether you're like
Bathsheba or me or or or the king and then that that that
that that would be fair.

Mitch   I'm pretty sure the king doesn't have to do
jury duty /

Duggan   Or, maybe, it could be like one huge rota system!
Where we all have to do all the shit jobs for a bit, but then
we get to do all the nice jobs for a bit. Like you'd spend six
weeks doing this or going to war or slaughtering animals,
but then, *then,* you'd get to swim with dolphins or play with
children or host a daytime TV quiz show about . . . (*Finding
the word.*) clouds! Because that would be fair! And . . . maybe
I should write a book! Yes! A book exposing the reality of
everything! And it will be about things like *this* and people
like *us* and a society like *ours* and the book will be a . . .
rom-com!

Beat.

Mitch   It doesn't sound very romantic.

Beat.

Yaz   OK, I'm gonna go.

Duggan   Please stay.

Yaz   Why?

Duggan Just . . . stay here. Urm. I'll be five minutes. Will you both still be here in five minutes?

Yaz Urm. Sure.

Duggan I'll be right back.

Duggan *rushes off.*

Beat. They look at each other.

Mitch So . . . he's got a full-time job?

Yaz I guess so.

Mitch How does *he* have a full-time job? (*Beat.*) There was a guy in my class at school who once lied about having Crohn's disease. This feels a bit like that.

Beat.

Yaz OK, so yeah, I'm gonna go.

Mitch OK. Yeah.

Yaz Yeah.

Mitch I think I will too.

Yaz Cool.

They grab their bags. **Yaz** *turns to leave.*

Mitch (*to* **Yaz**) What are you doing now?

She turns back to **Mitch**.

Yaz I'm just gonna go home.

Mitch I didn't mean to be such a prick by the way.

Yaz No, it's cool.

Beat.

Mitch Well, this maybe could be the last one of these, so, I don't know, like if you want to keep seeing each other or . . .

Yaz Oh, uhm . . .

Mitch   Coz like, if I'm not getting paid then you're like the only good thing that's actually come out of this for me.

Yaz   Urm . . . yeah. Sorry, I, yeah . . . I really don't want that.

Mitch   Oh.

Yaz   Yeah, sorry.

Mitch   No, of course – that's OK.

Beat.

Yaz   Bye.

Mitch   Bye.

She leaves. **Mitch** *is left alone on stage. He hates himself in this moment. He might cry. He doesn't. He waits for a moment and then leaves through the same door.*

The stage is empty for a few seconds.

Duggan *emerges with three boxes of pizza stacked on top of each other.*

Duggan (*singing from off stage*)   When the moon hits your eye, like a big pizza pie . . .

He stops singing when he sees that everyone's gone. He doesn't know where to sit. After a moment, he sits down on one of the chairs. Maybe he stands up and sits down on the floor instead.

He opens the box. He doesn't look impressed. He closes the box.

He stares up at the cameras in the corners of the room. He nods to each one.

Dr Eavis *comes in, sees* **Duggan** *sat there.*

Dr Eavis   What are you doing?

Duggan   Oh, hey. I was just, urm . . . I think everyone else's gone.

Dr Eavis   Yeah.

Duggan   But I uh . . .

Beat.

I got pizza.

Beat. Suddenly panicked.

Is that OK?

Dr Eavis   Yeah. That's fine.

Beat.

Duggan   Sorry, do you need the room?

Dr Eavis   Urm, no, not really. But I did say you can go home, didn't I?

Duggan   Yeah, you did.

Dr Eavis   OK. Yeah. I forget what I've told which . . . (*She sighs.*) What type of pizza is it?

Duggan   Oh, I ordered one with artichokes but this one's just margherita.

Pause.

Do you want some?

Pause as **Dr Eavis** *is thinking. Then she nods her head.*

She sits down next to him. They eat pizza for a while.

Dr Eavis   I am a real doctor, by the way.

Duggan   Oh, yeah I know, we were just being . . . mean.

Dr Eavis   Like, yeah, I quit. But I've done all the training. I passed all the exams. Now I just pick up shifts like this, when I can.

Duggan   Right.

Dr Eavis   It's twice the pay for half the work.

Duggan   That's great.

Dr Eavis   It *is* great!

Beat. They eat.

Duggan   Was it all just a bit much then?

Dr Eavis   What?

Duggan   As in, just too much stress, too much death being a doctor.

Dr Eavis   No. Well yes, but no, it was . . . I mean I didn't mind all that. I've never been squeamish and I like working hard. I stopped because, well I mean, it's ridiculous really but I stopped because I went through this breakup? And I couldn't, I just couldn't do it anymore. Like everyone goes through breakups but I just – I don't know what it was – I just couldn't do this one.

Duggan *nods. Continues to eat pizza.*

Dr Eavis   We'd been going out for like three years and then he moved to Japan for work and so we broke up. And I thought, OK well, we'll still be friends and then maybe one day . . . I thought, maybe one day we'll get back together when he comes back, or if we don't, well I won't care anymore because I'll be with somebody else and then a year went by and then two years and I was still like *in love* with him. He was with someone else by then, they had moved in together and I was still here like thinking about him a thousand times a day.

Dr Eavis *chews another mouthful of pizza. Swallows.*

Like, even when I was – I don't know – like in clinic or talking to like . . . bereaved families, the whole time I was just thinking about Joe. And then one day I just thought: I've got to see him, I've got to go and tell him how I feel or otherwise I'll die. So, I did this huge grand gesture thing and went to the airport and I spent all my savings on a plane ticket to Japan and I arrived and when he opened the door, he was completely shocked. He was like so, so shocked, and I was so shocked that I actually did it. And he said, 'What are you doing here?' and I was like, 'I've come to win you back'. And he laughed. And I said, 'No, I'm serious', and he . . . Well, he was really kind about the whole thing actually. Him and his girlfriend. They let me stay the night. For a few nights actually. Then he called my parents and they called me and convinced me to come home. And then, when I got home, I didn't want to be a doctor anymore. Anyway, now, I just pick up shifts like this. Because I'm in debt, from leaving my proper job and from the flights.

Pause.

Duggan *turns to her.*

Duggan   Are we gonna kiss?

Dr Eavis *looks at him confused.*

Beat.

Dr Eavis (*kindly*)   No.

Beat.

Duggan   Yeah. Best not.

Duggan *continues to eat pizza.*

Lights change.

Dr Eavis *addresses the audience.*

Dr Eavis   When Duggan finished eating, I told him to go home.

Beat.

Week five.

She disappears.

Five

Mitch is sat alone. A moment. Yaz walks in. When she sees it's just Mitch, her energy changes. She sits down a few seats away from him.

Yaz I wasn't sure we'd be coming back.

Mitch Same.

Pause.

Did you get my message by the way?

Yaz Which one?

Mitch The one saying I was sorry.

Yaz Oh. Yeah. I think so.

Beat.

Mitch I obviously do care more about Bathsheba being OK than getting paid.

Yaz OK.

Mitch I was just stressed.

Yaz OK.

Mitch And being an idiot.

Yaz Yeah.

Mitch And I was thinking about it during the week and I've been thinking . . . sorry, am I talking to much about myself?

Yaz Urm. I mean. Sort of, but . . . you've started now.

Mitch OK. And so, yeah, I was sort of thinking about it all during the week and I've been thinking that maybe it's time for me to just . . . opt out. You know. For a bit. Like, the other day I met this guy at a party who's like one of these freeganism types? He like squats in an oligarch's mansion and he eats out of a literal bin and he grows potatoes in the park and steals clothes from mannequins he finds in skips and he was telling me that he's not actually *that* unhappy. (*Beat.*) So, yeah, I might do that for a bit. I don't know.

Yaz   Don't do that.

Beat.

Mitch   No. I won't.

Yaz   Good.

Mitch   I was like . . . joking or something.

Beat.

Mitch   So, what about you? What are you gonna do now?

Yaz   Urm. I've been looking into retaking some exams. I'm thinking of going travelling . . . But, yeah, my godmum . . . she actually thinks she can get me a job doing admin here for a few months. So, I might do that. For a bit.

Mitch   Right. Nice. That sounds like a nice idea.

Duggan *enters.*

Duggan   Wazza!

Yaz *and* **Mitch** *are startled. They do not match* **Duggan**'s *energy. He deflates.*

Yaz   Hey.

Duggan *goes to sit down.*

Duggan   How are you guys?

Yaz   Fine, thanks.

Mitch   Yeah, fine.

Pause.

Yaz   How's the book coming along?

Duggan   Oh right. Yeah. It's getting there. Haven't started writing yet. Still in the research phase. But I'm glad I'm doing it, I think it's important. In fact, maybe it'll be better as a podcast. (*Turns to* **Mitch**.) Actually Mitch, do you wanna go twos on this pod?

Mitch   I'll . . . think about it.

Bathsheba *enters. Her arm's in a sling. They don't notice her.*

Bathsheba   Hello.

They turn around.

Yaz   Hey /

Mitch   Hi /

Yaz   Oh my god /

Duggan   What happened to you?

Beat.

Bathsheba   'It's more likely you'll get hurt on the way to the trial than as a participant.'

Pause.

All   Fuck.

Duggan   So, what, you . . . ?

Bathsheba   I got hit by a car.

Duggan   Fuck off, really?!

Bathsheba   I was on my way here last week, when a car came out of nowhere.

Yaz   And so, you broke your . . . ?

Bathsheba   My elbow. In three places.

Duggan   Are elbows . . . can they break in three places?

Bathsheba   Mine did.

Dr Eavis *marches in.*

Dr Eavis   Hello, sorry for the delay. It's so great to see all of you. Welcome back, Ms Binks.

Duggan   Ms Binks?

Bathsheba   That's my surname.

Duggan   Sorry, so your name is Bathsheba *Binks*?

Bathsheba   Yes.

Duggan   Well, Mitch, that's not gonna work for the podcast, everyone will think we've made it up.

Dr Eavis   So. Just a few more hours and then we'll all be wrapped up. Uhm . . . So yeah. (*Beat.*) Well done for getting through it. You all turned up, that's the main thing. That's what we mainly look for in our participants really, the turning up. And uh . . . yeah, so from everyone here I'd just like to say: (*Gathers herself, breathes in.*) thank you. Thank you for helping to contribute to scientific knowledge. You should all be very proud.

Smiles.

I'll be back this afternoon to take blood. Do your obs. And then . . . (*In an overly affected Southern drawl.*) then y'all are free to roam the prairie!

Smiles. Beat. She doesn't know why she said that.

Oh. Out of interest, did anyone find love?

Beat.

Yaz *and* **Mitch** *shuffle in their chairs.*

Dr Eavis   Yeah. I made up that story at the start. No one falls in love at a worms trial!

She smiles.

Alright. Pop your pills, they're (*Points to the table.*) sur la table. Some French for you there. La Française. French French French. Love the French! (*Quick flash of realisation.*) French!

They're French next door. Oh my god, they're French. Right, well, I definitely have got some apologies to make.

She turns to go.

Bathsheba   Dr Eavis. (**Dr Eavis** *turns back*.) What will these drugs be used for?

Dr Eavis   Oh, the drug's for anxiety.

Mitch/Duggan/Yaz/Bathsheba   Ohh . . .

Dr Eavis   That *was* in the literature, that was literally on the first page . . .

They all look a bit sheepish.

Dr Eavis   Did *none* of you read the literature?!

They shake their heads. She sighs.

Duggan   *turns to the others.*

Duggan   Seriously?!

Yaz, Mitch and **Bathsheba** *look faintly guilty.*

Dr Eavis   I'll be back later. To say a proper au revoir.

She leaves. The participants get up to take the pills.

Bathsheba *starts filling in one of the forms.*

Duggan   Have you got a side effect *already*?

Bathsheba   I think so. I'm just a bit hot. Mainly my face. But . . . no, everywhere actually. It's like a fuzz. Like everything's vibrating really . . . well. (*Reading the top of the form.*) Hm. Salvinorin A. Did you all know that?

Duggan   Know what?

Bathsheba   Salvinorin A. That's the drug we're trialling. Microdosing.

Duggan   Oh.

Bathsheba   It's psychoactive.

Beat.

I've only ever done one psychoactive trial before. It was the first trial I ever did. (*Beat.*) There was this old man there and he told me that you get two types of participants: the ones who do psychoactive trials and the ones who refuse. He had a word for the ones that did them, he called us brainsluts. He told me he'd worked on a fishing trawler for forty years. And that when he retired, and arrived back on land, he felt seasick for the very first time. He said the only time the sickness went away was when he lay in his girlfriend's arms and she put her hand over his eyes and rocked him back and forth. I've always taken that to mean something very specific and very beautiful. But now, looking back on it, I think he was probably just quite high.

Pause.

Duggan Bathsheba.

She looks at him.

Would you lead us in a guided meditation?

She thinks for a moment. Beat.

Bathsheba OK.

Duggan Should we all do a line each? Like last time?

She nods. **Bathsheba** *takes a deep breath in. They all put their hands on their knees and close their eyes.*

Bathsheba Imagine you arrive at an old, beautiful house. Maybe it's somewhere you haven't been since you were a child or maybe you've never been there before. You push open the front door and walk through the hallway. The floorboards creak. (*Beat.*) You breathe in. You breathe out. Mitch?

Mitch Uhm. You breathe in and you smell . . . its smell. And it's . . . it's smelly. It's a really smelly old house. (*Beat.*) It smells of damp and . . . rosemary.

Bathsheba Yaz?

Yaz   Uhm . . . you push open the next door and you're in the kitchen now and it's full of . . . flowers. Like the house plants have taken over. There are bluebells growing in the sink. And maybe a squirrel lives in the kettle and a real cuckoo has built its nest in a cuckoo clock. Or no, maybe that's too much.

Beat.

Bathsheba   Duggan?

At some point during **Duggan***'s next line, soft music starts to play. For this moment, I like The Velvet Underground's 'Ride into the Sun – "1969" / 2014 Mix'. The music should continue until the end of the play.*

Duggan   And so, yeah . . . you walk through the kitchen-forest-place-thing and you get to the back door and you open it and there's a garden. A normal garden this time. And in the garden, you can see some . . . strangers. You see the sun shining down on their faces, and you smile at them. (*Beat.*) And they smile at you. (*Beat.*) And for a moment, everything feels OK.

Lights change.

Dr Eavis *walks downstage. Addresses the audience.*

Dr Eavis   At 10:59, the Wi-Fi came back on and so, for the next six hours, Yaz, Mitch and Duggan scrolled through their phones and Bathsheba continued to bead.

Then at 5pm, I told them they could all go home. Duggan asked if anyone wanted to go to the pub. They said, 'Maybe not tonight. Soon though.'

End of play.